Gregor Kirchhofer

Why Are Horror Games Appealing?

Anchor Academic
Publishing

Kirchhofer, Gregor: Why Are Horror Games Appealing?, Hamburg, Anchor Academic Publishing 2017

Buch-ISBN: 978-3-96067-109-1
PDF-eBook-ISBN: 978-3-96067-609-6
Druck/Herstellung: Anchor Academic Publishing, Hamburg, 2017

Bibliografische Information der Deutschen Nationalbibliothek:
Die Deutsche Nationalbibliothek verzeichnet diese Publikation in der Deutschen Nationalbibliografie; detaillierte bibliografische Daten sind im Internet über http://dnb.d-nb.de abrufbar.

Bibliographical Information of the German National Library:
The German National Library lists this publication in the German National Bibliography. Detailed bibliographic data can be found at: http://dnb.d-nb.de

All rights reserved. This publication may not be reproduced, stored in a retrieval system or transmitted, in any form or by any means, electronic, mechanical, photocopying, recording or otherwise, without the prior permission of the publishers.

Das Werk einschließlich aller seiner Teile ist urheberrechtlich geschützt. Jede Verwertung außerhalb der Grenzen des Urheberrechtsgesetzes ist ohne Zustimmung des Verlages unzulässig und strafbar. Dies gilt insbesondere für Vervielfältigungen, Übersetzungen, Mikroverfilmungen und die Einspeicherung und Bearbeitung in elektronischen Systemen.

Die Wiedergabe von Gebrauchsnamen, Handelsnamen, Warenbezeichnungen usw. in diesem Werk berechtigt auch ohne besondere Kennzeichnung nicht zu der Annahme, dass solche Namen im Sinne der Warenzeichen- und Markenschutz-Gesetzgebung als frei zu betrachten wären und daher von jedermann benutzt werden dürften.

Die Informationen in diesem Werk wurden mit Sorgfalt erarbeitet. Dennoch können Fehler nicht vollständig ausgeschlossen werden und die Diplomica Verlag GmbH, die Autoren oder Übersetzer übernehmen keine juristische Verantwortung oder irgendeine Haftung für evtl. verbliebene fehlerhafte Angaben und deren Folgen.

Alle Rechte vorbehalten

© Anchor Academic Publishing, Imprint der Diplomica Verlag GmbH
Hermannstal 119k, 22119 Hamburg
http://www.diplomica-verlag.de, Hamburg 2017
Printed in Germany

Abstract

This paper tries to explore why so many people actively seek out and enjoy horror as a form of entertainment. Why some find pleasure in horror is a question that many have asked themselves before, but never fully answered. This paper does not claim to deliver a general answer to that question, but rather offers an overview of the most popular theories and hypotheses, as well as a study focusing on the player affect. The explanations and solutions offered include mostly psychological, emotional or general approaches. Every approach presented has its benefits and flaws and will be discussed accordingly. How these come into play individually, as well as in connection to each other, will be a major part of this paper. After having provided the general theoretical basis of horror and why it might be so appealing to some people, this paper will go on discussing the medium game, and in a further step, try to explore if the unique characteristics of the medium game changes the overall horror experience one might have. Different aspects and properties of the medium in question will be discussed in detail. How immersion affects us as consumers, what the role of interactivity is and how they both relate to one another in-game. How this understanding comes into play in a game design context and how it can create a whole different experience for the player. And lastly, how certain game design elements can be utilized to further improve the emotional response.

keywords: horror, videogame, why horror, game design, paradox, appeal

Contents

Introduction	5
Meta-Emotions, Catharsis and the Need for Affect	6
Meta-Emotions	6
Catharsis	7
Transfer	9
Sensation Seeking	11
The Shadow, the Monster and the Curiosity	14
C.G. Jung's Shadow and the Collective Unconscious	14
Carroll's Monster and the Curiosity	18
The Paradox of the Heart	19
The Video Game	24
Immersion	24
Interactivity	25
Survival Horror Games	27
Conclusion	30
Bibliography	31

Introduction

At the beginning of my research for this paper, I was not sure if anyone else ever asked the question, why horror achieved such popularity and what it is that makes people want to experience such entertainment over and over, in a scientific context. I was very curious about that question myself, which is also why I chose to commit to this question despite probable complications such as lack of research or no solid results. As a fan of such entertainment, I was positively surprised to find out that there had been some interest raised around that topic before. In the end, one of the biggest challenges was not the lack of sources and research about that topic, but rather the almost philosophical nature of the topic, which presented itself during my research. More than a handful of thinkers, academics and experts wrote about this seemingly paradoxical phenomenon behind horror entertainment, but the acquired knowledge is far from consistent. Many theories and hypotheses have been published, focusing on all kinds of different aspects of the whole subject matter. Yet, precisely because of that wide array of different starting points, it seems like the individual theories are detached from one another. Mostly presenting one solution for one particular aspect but never being able to find a truly general explanation. And so far, at least according to my research, no theory that can explain every aspect about the fascination of horror has been found yet. Apart from the question why horror entertainment is so appealing to certain people, I was equally curious if the medium game might have a different effect on the horror experience for the end consumer than other media and how this is achieved.

Meta-Emotions, Catharsis and the Need for Affect

To start my search for different theories that might help explaining the mystery of why we enjoy the experience we get from a good horror story, I want to discuss catharsis, as well as other theories that use emotions in their explanation models, and explain why it might be a relevant aspect when trying to answer the overall question of this paper.

Meta-Emotions

When we talk about emotions and start thinking about how much we actually know about our emotions, it becomes soon clear that it is a rather abstract concept which is hard to visualize or fully explain. The model of meta-emotions suggests that there is more than one emotional state we can find ourselves in at the same time. Every now and then, the emotions we experience at certain points in our lives appear more complex than others. Especially in the case of experiencing positive emotions as well as negative emotions at the same time. "Sometimes we wallow in sorrow; some pleasures are embittered with pains. Fears can be pleasant, and joys may be spoiled with regret" (C. Jäger, A. Bartsch, 2006). A very simple example to further illustrate the subject matter would be to enjoy a delicious piece of cake while feeling bad about not sticking to or even cheating on ones diet. It soon becomes apparent that there is something paradoxical about the emotions we feel.

When enjoying something you're not supposed to or feeling sad about something that is actually making you feel mainly happy, it becomes clear that emotions can manifest themselves in the most interesting combinations. Furthermore, that means that we have the ability to direct emotions towards other emotions, or in other words, the way we feel about how we feel. "We shall call such higher-order emotions meta-emotions." They way these meta-emotions come into play and how they are elicited is yet to be researched in greater depth. Nevertheless there are a few interesting investigations made on account of meta-emotions (C. Jäger, A. Bartsch, 2006).

Catharsis

The term "catharsis" has existed for more than two millenniums now. It was first used by the Greek philosopher Aristotle back in the ancient Greece. The linguistic origin of that term can be found in the greek word "Katharsis" which means as much as purification or purgation. Aristotle used this term to explain why people were enjoying tragic theatre plays such as *Oedipus the King*. Unfortunately, the exact definition of the word catharsis has never been specified. Over the past centuries, it has always been heavily debated what the true meaning is. Nevertheless, it is mostly believed that it refers to a cleansing or purification of emotions when experiencing a controlled tragic event, for instance in form of a theatre such as the one mentioned above. This means that the spectator is identifying herself or himself with the actor and is feeling the portrayed emotions as if they were real and their own. The spectator can then exercise her or his own anxiety, fear and terror through them. This allows her or him to direct the negative emotions outwards and furthermore experience the purifying effect of catharsis. Other critics also see catharsis as a form of moral lesson that allows one to experience extreme fictional scenarios which in the end serves as reference (Howard, n.d.; Nightingale, 2006; Catharsis, n.d.).

As simple and coherent or compelling this theory might seem at a first glance, there are definitely some weak points that are worth mentioning. Firstly, the cathartic effect theory assumes that the main motivation to want to witness a tragic event (theatre, movie, game etc.) is to release negative emotions throughout the process of experiencing them. Yet the question presents itself if the emotions being referred to are not actually created by experiencing whatever tragic event in the first place. This would mean that the emotions created by the experience and the ones who are claimed to be purged through the cathartic effect cannot be the same, and therefore, purging or releasing these negative emotions in question cannot be regarded as the only nor the main motivation behind the craving of experiencing horror. One might refer to these negative emotions that catharsis is supposed to purge as all the negative emotions that had been accumulated over a certain period of time, which then on the other hand would contradict its applicability to what we know as contemporary horror or "art-horror" as Noël Carroll would refer to it.

Nevertheless, its theoretical approach might well play an important role in the general theoretical process behind answering the question why we enjoy horror in the first place. Even if the theory might be proven wrong, it still functions as a piece of the bigger puzzle or as a foundation for other more elaborate theories to build upon on.

Transfer

And this is exactly where the excitation transfer theory comes into play, utilizing aspects of the catharsis hypothesis while finding supposedly better or at least more promising solutions to the overall applicability of the theory. The transfer model is based on what Dolf Zillermann calls the Mood-Management-Theory, which he has developed in the 1970s. In his work, Zillermann advocates the importance of hedonistic behaviorism and their effects. In other words, it states that the most important factors concerning our behavior and the reasons why we do, or not do certain things, is driven by the simple motivation of maximizing the gratifying reward of the positive emotions we feel. This concept would then for example be able to explain, to some degree at least, why we do certain things over others and therefore, why we choose to experience certain forms of media entertainment. In a further step, the theory suggests that the emotional gratification one experiences is dependent on the individual's arousal level, induced by what we experience. Which means that a low arousal level evokes a less intense emotional experience than the one achieved by a very high arousal level.

When we apply this thought process now onto experiences such as the ones horror entertainment provides, and keep what we know about the cathartic effect and the concept of meta-emotions in mind, it reveals the surface of what the excitation transfer theory tries to illustrate. Assuming that watching a horror movie then invokes some extremely negative emotions seems to make little sense at first considering the hedonistic motivation basis used here. But, when focusing on the gratifying and rewarding overflow of positive emotions after the spectator sees the plot resolve itself, suddenly provides a completely different perspective on the subject matter. If we now, in a further step, consider that the more intense the emotional experience is, the stronger the joyful emotions are, it might as well explain why audiences and producers of horrifying entertainment always try to push the limits further and further in order to provide constantly increasing horrifying images (Jäger & Bartsch, 2006; Kunczik, 2006).

Seeing how the transfer theory utilizes fear and the emotional relief that follows it when watching tragic or horrifying imagery, the resemblance to the earlier discussed catharsis hypothesis becomes more apparent. The most notable difference between the two approaches though, lies in what kind of fear is referred to. The catharsis hypothesis only refers to a pre-existing fear that has, on its own, not directly anything to do with whatever form of entertainment that is being consumed. It implies that the fear, which serves as motivation, has already formed itself before the individual decides to watch a tragic play (or any other form of tragic, horrifying form of entertainment) and that the need to release or purge that fear is the reason why the individual would go in the first place. The excitation transfer approach, on the other hand, does not expect an already pre-existing fear but refers to whatever fear is emerging during the process of watching a tragic play (or any other form of tragic, horrifying form of entertainment). Therefore, what is referred to as one of the biggest flaws of the catharsis hypothesis, is not only being avoided but explained in different and more relatable way. Having the emotional state which is required for the catharsis hypothesis to work might not be something everyone has ever experienced first hand, or is even able to relate and identify with. But nearly everyone has already made the experience of a sudden, exciting rush of adrenaline one might get watching a scary movie, playing a stomach twisting game or even riding rollercoasters and the very comfortable feeling of relief that follows such an experience. All these feelings occur in the process of doing these things and are mostly inevitable (Jäger & Bartsch, 2006). Of course one might argue that not everyone is actively seeking out such intense experiences. A lot of people would do everything in their power to avoid any kind of extremes. Glen Sparks, a professor of communication who studies the effect of media on people says that only about one-third of people actively seek out these intense experiences. Another third actively tries to avoid any kind of extreme situations, while the last third occupies a sort of middle ground, where they do occasionally seek out such entertainment and also enjoy it, but only to a certain degree (Sparks, n.d.).

Sensation Seeking

Why people seem to handle the desire for such forms of entertainment in such different ways has to do with their NFA, or need for affect, as Anne Bartsch, Markus Appel, and Dennis Storch called it in their paper "Predicting Emotions and Meta-Emotions at the Movies: The Role of the Need for Affect in Audiences' Experience of Horror and Drama".

The concept of the need for affects is again widely utilizing the idea of meta-emotions and tries to shed more light onto the question why some people enjoy intense media content while other people seem to show no motivation to seek such content out whatsoever. "The NFA is defined as the 'general motivation of people to approach or avoid situations and activities that are emotion inducing for themselves and others'" (Bartsch, Appel & Storch, 2010, p170). It is a conceptual property attributed to every individual and takes into account "moods, emotions, preferences, and related evaluations" (Bartsch et al., 2010, p170). According to that idea, all individuals have a certain desire for emotional affect in their lives. If the NFA is high, then that person will actively seek out whatever extreme experience that provides enough distress to satisfy the initial NFA. On the other hand, an individual which has a low NFA will try to keep their emotional state stable and avoid anything too exciting. Applying the concept of NFA might also hint at why phenomenons such as genre preferences become so apparent (Bartsch et al., 2010).

A very similar approach as the one just explained involving the need for affect is being referred to as sensation seeking. It appears to utilize very similar concepts, which is why its' mentioning is appropriate at this point.

Research on ‚sensation seeking' suggests that strong emotions can satisfy a desire for salient and intense experience. (...) The strength of the sensation seeking motive has been shown to influence subject's emotional preferences. Sensation seekers preferred emotionally intense media stimuli, regardless of whether these elicited positive or negative emotions. Participants with a weak sensation seeking motive, by contrast, preferred neutral and positive stimuli. (Jäger & Bartsch, 2006)

In a field study conducted by Anne Bartsch, Markus Appel, and Dennis Storch, the results were meant to find out more about how the different levels of NFA affected the emotional experiences of the spectators, some remarkable findings have been made. According to the study, a high NFA resulted in an amplification of the emotional experience. Therefore, negative emotions felt by individuals with a higher NFA were stronger and more intense then the ones experienced by individuals with a lower NFA. Furthermore, it appears that a high NFA also allows for a more positive evaluation on the level of meta-emotions. Which means that although the negative emotions felt by individuals with a high NFA are worse, the way these individuals thought about them and resolved them on a meta-emotional level was proportionally more positive and rewarding.

"Besides heightened levels of emotional reactivity we found evidence that the NFA was related to a more positive evaluation of emotions in terms of meta-emotion." In other words, individuals who have a high NFA and therefore have a strong emotional experience, seem to be more acceptant towards their feelings. On the other hand, the other side of the NFA spectrum appears to enjoy their emotional responses to intense experiences far less and also find their emotions "less normatively adequate" (Bartsch et al., 2010).

The Shadow, the Monster and the Curiosity
C.G. Jung's Shadow and the Collective Unconscious

Carl Gustav Jung believes that the human mind possesses something he called collective unconscious, a common foundation of psychological archetypes that every human being shares with each other regardless of what cultural, social or personal experiences and memories. One of these archetypes is the one referred to as the shadow. The construct of the shadow is a very interesting concept which has been an anchor point for many theories apart from the one I am about to present. C. G. Jung was a doctor and a psychoanalyst in Zurich who strongly believed that utilizing the concept of the shadow and working with it is a major part of his work with patients, their mind and himself as a psychoanalyst. He characterized the shadow as being a partly conscious and partly unconscious aspect present in our mind. This Jungian archetype represents the darkest side in us which contains the irrational, instinctive and least desirable aspects in our personality which we try to hide because of societal reasons, self esteem or simply out of shame. It implies that every individual is ridden by the same sinister urges locked away deep inside the unconscious. It is according to him one of the archetypes which influences us the most. Not only does it influence us but it also holds the power to create a conflict which in the end can prevent us to react or push us to do a variety of unexpected or maybe even unwanted actions. It is also important to state that this archetype is certainly not a trait which is acquired over time by specific individuals due to certain experiences they might have made in their lives, but is given from the very beginning, it is part of each and every one of us. Its major difference lies in the way it presents itself, how it influences us and of course what consequences the outcome holds. Furthermore, Jung clearly mentions that the shadow's character is highly driven from the individuals subconscious which makes it especially valuable for psychoanalysis. It consists mainly of unwanted and repressed facets of our personality which are not necessarily bad or wrong but don't conform to society, moral standards or other expectations of how people should behave and what they should not do (Jung, 1992).

Since the shadow represents everything we don't want to be as well as everything we should not be, it is hard to identify with that concept. This is why our mind is projecting the shadow onto our environment, or in other words onto the people who surround us. The process of projection allows us to disconnect ourselves from the shadow and percept it in a different way (Storch, 1996).

This change of perspective now allows the individual to diagnose and confront the shadow. Most of the time this process is accompanied by a strong sense of resistance by the individual and can turn out to not be an easy task. But according to Jung, it is important to go through that process of discovery and fight against the shadow to successfully implement the collective unconscious into our every day lives and create room for the up to this point undiscovered shadow in order to develop the positive aspects of this archetype.

To specify the importance of integrating the shadow into the understanding of our mind and what positive aspects can derive from this practice, we have to understand the consequences of deciding not to acknowledge this darker side of ours. The less contact the conscious and the unconscious have, the more undesirable personality aspects are being suppressed by the individual, the more these aspects risk to amplify themselves in severity before finally breaking out. This outbreak on the other hand just pushes the individual into suppressing and containing it even more since whatever consequences this emergence of the shadow might have provoked is most likely not going to receive positive attention or even approval. In many cases, a common reaction would be disapproval, fear and shame which then turns into denial when it comes to admitting that the shadow is a part of ones mind in the first place (Storch, 1996).

A little further in Carl Gustav Jung's book, he uses a fictional story of a very calm and introverted father, who against everyone's expectations, one day suddenly murders his wife and children before taking his own life as an example to further illustrate his thoughts. He then comments on these unfortunate consequences of denying the existence of the shadow with the following words:

Es ist oft tragisch, zu sehen, auf wie durchsichtige Weise ein Mensch sich selber und anderen das Leben verpfuscht, aber um alles in der Welt nicht einsehen kann, inwiefern die ganze Tragödie von ihm selber ausgeht und von ihm selber immer wieder aufs Neue genährt und unterhalten wird. Sein Bewusstsein tut es allerdings nicht, denn es jammert und flucht über eine treulose Welt, die sich in immer weitere Ferne zurückzieht. Es ist vielmehr ein unbewusster Faktor, der die welt- und selbstverhüllenden Illusionen spinnt. Das Gespinst zielt in der Tat auf einen Kokon hin, in welchem das Subjekt am Ende eingeschlossen ist. (Jung, 1992, p.19)

Even Stephen King talks about this unconventional relationship with horror in his letter "Why We Crave Horror Movies". He describes a very similar if not identical phenomenon concerning the influences and effects, that also Jung's shadow archetype addresses, without ever referring to Jung in any sort of way whatsoever. King believes that every one of us is "mentally ill" and it is just a question of how much of it we are showing that discloses the truth about ourselves to the people around us. Therefore it also makes perfect sense to him to enjoy the morbid, the horrifying and the gruesome in whatever form it may present itself, although it might seem like something we shouldn't want. The people who appear to us as normal and sane basically exercise their need for the morbid and the abnormal in a better way according to King.

> *The potential lyncher is in almost all of us (excluding saints, past and present; but then, most saints have been crazy in their own ways), and every now and then, he has to be let loose to scream and roll around in the grass.* (King, n.d.)

While growing up, our parents, social environment and society teach us what is normal and what is abnormal, what is good and what is bad. However well this learning phase shaped us as individuals, we sometimes still have theses desires to do things we perfectly well know should not be things that we are supposed to crave for. Yet, these "anticivilization emotions don't go away, and they demand periodic exercise" (King, n.d.). This is where the horror as a form of entertainment finds its place and comes into play. It appeals with its specific characteristics "to all that is worst in us" and finds our "nastiest fantasies realized" (King, n.d.).

But all of this certainly does not mean that we are necessarily bad, sick or abnormal people. Finding joy in horror and feeding these anti-civilized emotions is just one way to keep them under control and not let them overwhelm us (King, n.d.).

Carroll's Monster and the Curiosity

Noël Carroll is a distinguished professor of philosophy who has attracted quite some attention around the end of the last century with his fresh approaches on some heavily discussed philosophical matters. His academic interests include mostly aesthetic theory, the philosophy of visual arts and the philosophy of emotions, but he also offered some new perspectives concerning the paradoxes of horror as a form of entertainment. This was achieved thanks to the publication of his book "The Philosophy of Horror - Paradoxes of the Heart" in 1990. Especially the chapter "Why Horror" has fueled a number of debates in the past years among which Andrew Tudor and his work turned out to be a very important intellectual asset, building upon Carroll's text about why we might enjoy horror the way we do (Noël Carroll, n.d.).

Tudor, an academic who has proven himself most respected in that particular field, explains in his response article to Carroll's text "Why Horror" in what ways Carroll's approach is different and why it sheds a new light onto the scope of the debates about the controversies of horror as a form of entertainment. Up till then, most attempts to find a general explanation concerning these paradox phenomenons were based on psychoanalytic theories among some which were directly drawn from Freud's scientific achievements such as the 'return of the repressed' and 'the uncanny'. Others used psychoanalytical concepts to "explore the ways in which unconscious structures forms of representation." (Tudor, 1997) However, most attempts to find a general answer are "insufficiently specific" and do not succeed to take into account the big variety of individuals, their own characteristics and predispositions towards horror properly.

Explanations such as the ones presented by Carroll and Tudor himself are more centered on the audience as individuals and their personal experience and relationship with the appeal of horror. But while it might be a different approach to the problematic, the question is still far from being answerable. Tudor points out that one of the biggest challenges is the insufficient amount of solid evidence which forces philosophers and other thinkers to base their thoughts and argumentations on nothing more then speculations which experts can mostly not even agree on (Tudor, 1997).

The Paradox of the Heart

In his book "the philosophy of horror - paradoxes of the heart", Carroll is exploring a new explanation of the appeal of horror which has proven to be one of the "clearest and most persuasive general attempts" (as mentioned above) according to Tudor. Especially interesting and absolutely mandatory for Carroll's explanation is his differentiation between horror and art-horror. Horror referring to real and truly horrifying experiences and art-horror being a fictional, man made emotional horror experience which aims to evoke a certain emotional discomfort in the spectators.

The weapons of the creators of such art-horror entertainment are according to Carroll a specific group of emotions that have to be conveyed in order to construct such amusement. Fear, disgust and repulsion, to be more specific, are the three emotions in question (Tudor, 1997).

These traits are, as Carroll wrote, also directly related to the features which a monster in such a story should possess. But these monsters on the other hand completely violate our understanding of cultural categories which is exactly where the paradox presents itself. Especially incomprehensible for Carroll is the fact that art-horror is not only a frightening experience but it is also meaning to provoke disgust and repulsion (Carroll, 1990).

> *We would not, for example, attempt to add some pleasure to a boring afternoon by opening the lid of a steamy trash can in order to savor its unwholesome stew of broken bits of meat, soldering fruits and vegetables, and noxious, unrecognisable clumps, riven thoroughly by all manner of crawling things.* (Carroll, 1990, p.158)

Yet the number of people who enjoy horror and are effectively seeking out that experience is so high that it is not to underestimate. Furthermore, this implies as well that if such a sum of people enjoy this form of entertainment, they cannot be considered abnormal or different but must be objectively referred to as normal people. "In short, there appears to be something paradoxical about the horror genre." (Carroll, 1990, p158)

The existence of this paradox becomes more clear when one considers the fact that horror obviously does have a certain kind of attraction towards its audience, yet its means to achieve this kind of attraction are the utilization of emotions that are intended to inflict disquiet, distress and displeasure. Considering these statements Carroll specifies the question "Why Horror?" and reformulates the question into "Why are horror audiences attracted by what, typically (in everyday life), should (and would) repel them?," or "How can horror audiences find pleasure in what by nature is distressful and unpleasant?" (Carroll, 1990, p. 159).

Carroll's general theory starts to take shape when you take into consideration the two, according to him, most important factors to the explanation of why we might enjoy horror, which is the monster of the narrative as well as the curiosity it evokes. With this monster figure, Carroll is not only referring to the classical monster or creature but more to a general idea of a monster figure within a horror narrative. When you consider what the right use of such a monster in a horror scenario is, then it becomes soon clear that "the monster is a functional ingredient in the type of narratives found in horror stories" (Carroll, 181). All narratives express a lot of their attraction in leaving the spectator to wonder how it continuous and especially how it will end. Yet in most realistically grounded stories there cannot be the same kind of curiosity which is evoked by the antagonist. These monsters are fictional and impossible beings, but these are precisely the reasons why they appear to be especially interesting to the audience. Usually the protagonists and the viewers have to go through a process referred to by Carroll as a process of discovery, disclosure and confirmation.

In the first part, the existence of an impossible being is discovered, something unknown to men and in most scenarios rather hostile. In a further step, properties characterizing the creature have to be discovered and informations about it gathered. All this helps in trying to understand more about that creature, whether it might be a demon, extraterrestrial, a ghost, created by the hands of a mad scientist or the result of the aftermath of a nuclear war. Knowing about the creatures then allows to proceed to the last step which is explaining and confirming its existence and furthermore, in many cases, figuring out how to fight it back, kill it, so that mankind would be saved once again and can continue prospering in peace. This whole process of discovery, disclosure and confirmation happens gradually, and even if the audience is given the key informations about the properties of the monster early on in the narrative, the protagonists will still have to go through the whole process by themselves. Because it happens gradually, it fuels our curiosity and our need to know in a way that we would even be willing to cope with the most unheard of gruesome and horror in order to find out. "Thus, to a large extent, the horror story is driven explicitly by curiosity" (Carroll, 1990, p.182). "Therefore, the disgust that such beings evince might be seen as part of the price to be paid for the pleasure of their disclosure" (Carroll, 1990, p.184).

To summarize these findings which might give a hint to why we like horror, Carroll states that there is obviously a relationship between the structures of art horror, horror narratives, the monster's characteristics and our need to satisfy our curiosity. It is also important to state that according to this theory, the main reason why we enjoy horror is that our need for revelation and the emotional reward that comes with satisfying this feeling of not knowing must be extremely strong. Yet it is not quite clear why we choose to be interested in such impossible scenarios and try to learn about fictional monsters. Carroll points out that similar narrative structures can also be found in other genres such as detective thrillers or disaster movies where the antagonist is neither impossible nor forcibly unknown. Yet the quality of the process of discovery, disclosure and confirmation in horror narratives must be at the very least a different one, if not a better one, because contrary to detective thrillers and disaster movies, it intentionally tries to test us and forces us to endure a certain amount of revulsion, disgust and distress before we are allowed the gratifying reward of knowing (Carroll, 1990).

Carroll's theory behind "why horror" promises a smooth and rather easy to understand approach to the whole problematic, yet even Carroll himself realizes that his theory is far from being impenetrable. The aspects his theory does better than most of the competing psychoanalytical approaches are at the same time also what shows the biggest flaw in Carroll's theory. Psychoanalytical theories and such using the unconscious (in example the one discussed above involving Carl Gustav Jung's shadow archetype) tend to be too specified and do not deliver a general enough explanation while also being too technical. Carroll's approach might provide a more general theory to why horror is appealing to us, yet it seems to restrict itself to a more general theory of why we find a very specific kind of horror appealing, therefore, it is not very versatile when it comes to all the different possible horror experiences one might have. Nevertheless, I have to say that especially the approach behind curiosity as the main motivation, even when isolated from the idea of monsters or impossible beings that violate our cultural categories, seems to be very promising and might be more generally applicable in combination with further future theories.

The Video Game

In this chapter I will attempt to discuss the medium game and its characteristics. I will be discussing the importance of aspects such as interactivity and immersion to the video game as a form of entertainment, as well as, in a later step, point out in what unique ways horror games differ from more common games. Ultimately, my goal is to find out if the affect of horror entertainment on the consumer or player is stronger or more intense when experienced in an interactive video game environment. Or in other words, if horror games could theoretically provide an even more intense and horrifying experience then other mediums, due to their immersive properties.

Immersion

DI Michael Großauer, professor and head of department at the *University of Applied Sciences* in Salzburg, AT, writes in his paper "Wirklichkeit.Fiktion.Immersion. Wirklichkeitskonstruktion im Computerspiel" about video games as a form of entertainment and explains what the unique properties of games are, as well as why they might be the most powerful medium yet.

The key aspect which lets video games stand out so much in comparison to other media is immersion. Immersion is a phenomenon which lets us completely focus on a specific task, plunging into a fictional world. Großauer even goes as far as to write of a detachment of the real world in order to completely accept the virtual reality we put ourselves into. Yet, another definition of the word immersion refers to it as a "Deep mental involvement in something" (Definition of immersion, n.d.). Immersion can of course also occur in other media (i.e. movies, books, storytelling etc.) but nowhere as effectively as in games. "Immersion ist ein wirklichkeitsgenerierender Vorgang, bei dem die Fiktion für die Zeit der Rezeption zu unserer Wirklichkeit wird" (Großauer, 2000, p.60). Our sense for time and space gets suspended, so that we can literally immerse into the virtual space. The detachment of our real world space is crucial yet it is not the only component to strong immersion. Realistic visualization of the fictional world in question is also essential. This does not only include how we perceive the environment visually but also the acoustic experience. Interactivity, though, is undoubtably the most important aspect to successful immersion in video games. Großauer states that even the most photorealistic graphical visualization cannot counter bad interactivity. The player, in order to immerse herself or himself successfully, is supposed to identify herself or himself with the controllable avatar or game character. As soon as the interaction between the player and the game seizes the immersion breaks. (Großauer, 2000)

Interactivity

What interactivity basically means is the interaction between human or player and the computer or system. It is an ongoing communication between the two just mentioned parties. This two-way process is what makes games so interesting. In no other medium can you experience this sort of dialogue between subject and medium. This dialogue lets the player change the course of her or his experience, individually guiding and directing the action and therefore truly interact with the medium game. This ability to provide the player with the power to decide for herself or himself how and in what ways he or she wants to advance the experience, is what makes games such a powerful medium. It makes interactivity the most important component of every good game, yet also the hardest to achieve well. How interactivity works within each game obviously varies from genre to genre, but often, developers try to hide poor interactivity behind amazing visuals, stunning sound effects and epic cut-scenes. They do this, trying to compensate for bad interactivity, but in most cases the quality of immersion suffers anyhow since its quality is directly related to the quality of the interaction. Movies and books only allow us to spectate and observe, the outcome and especially the process of getting there cannot be changed. It would not matter who or if even anyone watches the movie or reads the book, nothing about it would change. A game however, if providing everything necessary to feel truly immersed and being truly interactive, allows us to translate from being the spectator to being the actual protagonist, the one who pulls the strings and makes the decisions (Großauer, 2000).

Tanya Krzywinska, Professor in Digital Games and the Director of the *Games Academy* at *Falmouth University*, Cornwall, UK, offers a different approach to explain the fascination behind the medium game. In her paper, *Gaming Horror's Horror: Representation, Regulation, and Affect in Survival Horror Videogames* she states that:

> *A leading pleasure of games is that they provide an ordered, predictable system which affords players a multi-sensory, clearly demarcated affirmation of their skill, competency and autonomy, thereby providing a counterweight to an arbitrary, unpredictable and anxiety-inducing real world.* (Krzywinska, 2015, p.295)

In other words she thinks that a major motivation and success of the medium game derives from it being a way to escape the frightening real world. By providing the player with a believable fictional world that he or she can truly immerse herself or himself into, and by giving the player total control over her or his actions and her or his virtual fate, the game provides a more comfortable environment. It therefore serves as a kind of refuge, a world where things seems to be more simple. Not to mention that games usually wont put you in the shoes of yet another interchangeable and boring character. You get to be the hero, the one that saves the (fictional) world, the last man standing, or in short something extraordinary. Another aspect, especially true for competitive multiplayer games, is the "self-affirmation through the conduit of player performance" (Krzywinska, 2015, p.295). Finding pleasure in being the best at something or at least being better than someone else within the same rule system provided by the game. Overcoming challenges and competition in general is a crucial part to every game, whether it is against another player or the computer (Krzywinska, 2015).

Survival Horror Games

Considering what we have learned so far about the medium game, its characteristics and very unique properties, one might not agree with everything that has been said so far when thinking about the kind of experiences survival horror games provide. Survival horror games seem to purposely break some rules and do not follow key aspects of other game genres in order to achieve completely different gaming experiences. It effectively seeks out a way to trigger a different kind of player affect that one would usually expect in games. Instead of giving the player a feeling of dominance and control over the situation, survival horror games try to take precisely these aspects away in order to inflict emotions such as fear, terror, etc. These aspects boil down to something Tanya Krzywinska refers to as "giving agency to the player". Agency is what makes the player feel in control of herself or himself, the character and the environment in which he or she finds herself or himself. By taking away this agency the player becomes vulnerable, stripped of this sense of domination and superiority, which then leaves room for everything a good horror experience needs in order to give us that thrill we are looking for (Krzywinska, 2015).

One very practical example of a game utilizing the concept of taking away agency from the player would be *Silent Hill (1999)*. This classic among games took this concept very literal and works perfectly as an example. At certain points in the game, the game itself interferes with the players capabilities within the game by dulling her or his senses. Vision and visibility are obscured, lights turned down or completely off. Being blinded, the player has to focus more on what can be heard rather then what can be seen. But the atmospheric soundtrack and the well utilized sound effects such as undefinable cracking and growling will only further reinforce the players' uncertainty, fear and suspense (Krzywinska, 2015). How crucial the right utilization of sound is to create truly amazing and immersive horror experiences is often underestimated, but many experts agree on its importance.

> *Kombiniert mit realistischen Soundeffekten kann es bei diesen Spielen schon passieren, daß einem kalte Schauer über den Rücken laufen und der Puls schneller schlägt als sonst. Die Körpererfahrungen des realen Spielers werden benützt, um die Immersion zu intensivieren, gleichzeitig wird jedoch das explizite Wissen um den Körper ausgeschaltet.* (Großauer, 2000, p.73)

To further investigate the way horror affects the player and to further demonstrate the importance of suspense and its build up, I will present a recent study, conducted by Vanus Vachiratamporn, Roberto Legaspi, Koichi Moriyama, Masayuki Numao, which is trying to find evidence on how and in what ways the players are affected by horror games. A further motivation for conducting this experiment was to investigate "the possibility of bringing an affective gaming concept to the survival horror game genre" (An Investigation on Player Affect). During the experiment, the subjects, or players, were asked to play the horror game "Slender: The Eight Pages". While they were playing, the research group equipped them with EEG and EKG sensors. The information collected from these devices as well as the subject's input activity (keyboard and mouse) was acquired in order to be used to scientifically analyze possible correlations between the subject's level of affect and their play style. The results clearly presented the potential of EKG signals being utilized in the future in the context of horror gaming. Furthermore, the results suggest "that the suspense state has the most effect in maximizing the scariness of a game event" (An Investigation on Player Affect). Or in other words, the way the atmosphere, including sound, visuals and gameplay, is building up the suspense is crucial to an increased emotional response of the player. The better and the more intense the anticipation of the subject was, (which the EKG device was able to illustrate i.e. in form of heart rate) the stronger is the overall horror experience. This evidence, therefore, attempts to proof that (if desired to create even more extreme horror experiences) aspects such as anticipation and suspense, or in other words, the build-up, is more important then the actual (in game) horror climax (Vachiratamporn, Legaspi, Moriyama, & Numao, 2013).

Conclusion

In order to fully understand every aspect of horror and our affiliation to it, we cannot simply focus on only one approach. All of the approaches, theories and hypothesis discussed in this paper, present and explain a wide array of very interesting aspects concerning our relationship to horror. But they are only aspects, and nothing can always be said to be true. None of the presented approaches can provide a complete understanding on their own. However, if you perceive them as individual pieces of a bigger puzzle, a general understanding seems to present itself. Of course it is still far away from any complete explanation or even any general theory. Nevertheless, understanding everything we have learned so far proves to be a crucial component in understanding how horror games affect us. The combination between horror and the interactive, immersive nature of the video game turned out to be an especially interesting one. Whether the horror experience provided in a game is better than in other media or not, is still up for debate. But its uniqueness and difference when compared to any non-interactive entertainment became obvious. This statement appears clearer when taking into consideration the content of this research paper and assuming, for example, it is true that a high emotional response results in a more intense feeling of relief and reward, furthermore assuming that people who actively seek out this kind of entertainment always try to experience something even more extreme and assuming that video games, due to their immersive properties, really do provide a stronger emotional experience, it might explain why horror games experienced such a raise of popularity in the past years. The most important aspect for further research on this topic would probably be to not only focus on one aspect but to think more about the audience, their individual differences and predispositions towards the genre.

Bibliography

Bartsch, A., Appel, M., & Storch, D. (2010). Predicting Emotions and Meta-Emotions at the Movies: The Role of the Need for Affect in Audiences' Experience of Horror and Drama. Communication Research, 37(2), 167-190. doi:10.1177/0093650209356441

Catharsis. (n.d.). Retrieved June 2, 2016, from http://www.britannica.com/art/catharsis-criticism

Carroll, N. (1990). The philosophy of horror, or, Paradoxes of the heart. New York: Routledge.

Definition of immersion. (n.d.). Retrieved May 30, 2016, from http://www.oxforddictionaries.com/definition/english/immersion

Großauer, M., DI. (2000). Wirklichkeit.Fiktion.Immersion. Wirklichkeitskonstruktion im Computerspiel (Unpublished master's thesis). Salzburg, Techno-Z FH.

Howard, M. (n.d.). What is Catharsis? - Definition, Examples & History in Literature and Drama. Retrieved June 02, 2016, from http://study.com/academy/lesson/what-is-catharsis-definition-examples-history-in-literature-and-drama.html

Jung, C. G. (1992). Gesammelte Werke (8th ed., Vol. 9/2). Olten: Walter.

Jäger, C., & Bartsch, A. (2006). META-EMOTIONS. In Grazer Philosophische Studien (Vol. 73, pp. 179-204). Retrieved June 2, 2016, from https://www.uibk.ac.at/philtheol/jaeger/publ/meta-emotions-gps-73-homepage.pdf.

King, S. (n.d.). Why We Crave Horror Movies. Retrieved June 2, 2016, from
http://faculty.uml.edu/bmarshall/Lowell/whywecravehorrormovies.pdf

Krzywinska, T. (2015). Gaming Horrors Horror: Representation, Regulation, and Affect in Survival Horror Videogames. Journal of Visual Culture, 14(3), 293-297. doi:10.1177/1470412915607924

Kunczik, M., & Zipfel, A. (2006). Gewalt und Medien: Ein Studienhandbuch. Köln: Böhlau.

Nightingale, A. (2006). Literary theory and criticism: An Oxford guide (P. Waugh, Ed.). New York: Oxford University Press.

Noël Carroll. (n.d.). Retrieved June 2, 2016, from
http://www.gc.cuny.edu/Page-Elements/Academics-Research-Centers-Initiatives/Doctoral-Programs/Philosophy/Faculty-Bios/Noel-Carroll

Sparks, G. (n.d.). Why is Fear Fun? Retrieved May 24, 2016, from
http://news.discovery.com/human/psychology/fear-allure-halloween-121025.htm

Storch, M. (1996). Der Schatten als Ressource – psychodramatisches Aktionsreframing. In H. Hennig, et al. (Ed.), Kurzzeitpsychotherapie in Theorie und Praxis. Lenkerich: Pabst.

Tudor, A. (1997). Why Horror? The Peculiar Pleasures Of A Popular Genre. Cultural Studies, 11(3), 443-463. doi:10.1080/095023897335691

Vachiratamporn, V., Legaspi, R., Moriyama, K., & Numao, M. (2013). Towards the Design of Affective Survival Horror Games: An Investigation on Player Affect. 2013 Humaine Association Conference on Affective Computing and Intelligent Interaction. doi:10.1109/acii.2013.101

Vaughan, G. M., & Hogg, M. A. (2008). Social psychology. Harlow: Pearson Education Limited.